THE BATTLE OF GETTYSBURG
THE TURNING POINT IN
THE CIVIL WAR

THE BATTLE OF GETTYSBURG
THE TURNING POINT IN
THE CIVIL WAR

MASON CREST

Mason Crest
450 Parkway Drive, Suite D
Broomall, PA 19008
www.masoncrest.com

Cataloging-in-Publication Data on file with the Library of Congress.

Printed and bound in the United States of America.

First printing
9 8 7 6 5 4 3 2 1

ISBN: 978-1-4222-3884-4
Series ISBN: 978-1-4222-3881-3
ebook ISBN: 978-1-4222-7894-9
ebook series ISBN: 978-1-4222-7891-8

Produced by Regency House Publishing Limited
The Manor House
High Street
Buntingford
Hertfordshire
SG9 9AB
United Kingdom

www.regencyhousepublishing.com

Text copyright © 2018 Regency House Publishing Limited/Jonathan Sutherland
and Diane Canwell

PAGE 2: General Robert E. Lee

PAGE 3: Battlefield at Gettysburg National Military Park, Adams County, Pennsylvania.

RIGHT: Antietam, Maryland. Detective and Spy Allan Pinkerton with Abraham Lincoln and Major General John A. McClernand. Photographed at Antietam, Maryland, October 3, 1862.

PAGE 6: The Battle of Wilson's Creek Lithograph by Kurz & Allison, 1893.

CONTENTS

KEY ICONS TO LOOK FOR:

 Words to Understand: These words with their easy-to-understand definitions will increase the reader's understanding of the text, while building vocabulary skills.

 Sidebars: This boxed material within the main text allows readers to build knowledge, gain insights, explore possibilities, and broaden their perspectives by weaving together additional information to provide realistic and holistic perspectives.

 Educational Videos: Readers can view videos by scanning our QR codes, providing them with additional content to supplement the text. Examples include news coverage, moments in history, speeches, iconic sports moments, and much more!

 Text-Dependent Questions: These questions send the reader back to the text for more careful attention to the evidence presented here.

 Research Projects: Readers are pointed toward areas of further inquiry connected to each chapter. Suggestions are provided for projects that encourage deeper research and analysis.

 Series Glossary of Key Terms: This back-of-the-book glossary contains terminology used throughout the series. Words found here increase the reader's ability to read and comprehend high-level books and articles in this field.

OPPOSITE: Col. Alfred Duffie of the 1st Rhode Island Cavalry. Bull Run, Virginia.

Lincoln Memorial

The grand Lincoln Memorial is an American national monument built to honor the 16th President of the United States, Abraham Lincoln. It was designed by Henry Bacon, a New York architect. He had spent time studying in Europe where he was influenced and inspired by ancient Greek architecture. It was based on the architecture of a Greek temple. There are 36 Doric columns, each one representing one state of the U.S. at the date of President Lincoln's death.

The memorial contains a large seated sculpture of Abraham Lincoln. The nineteen-foot tall statue of Abraham Lincoln was designed by Daniel Chester French who was a leading sculptor from Massachusetts. The marble statue was carved in white Georgia marble by the Piccirilli brothers. The interior murals were painted by Jules Guerin. Ernest C. Bairstow created the exterior details with carvings by Evelyn Beatrice Longman. The memorial is inscribed with Lincoln's famous speech, "The Gettysburg Address." The words of the speech are etched into the wall to inspire all Americans just as it did in 1863. To the right is the entire Second Inaugural Address, given by Lincoln in March 1865. The memorial itself is 190 feet long, 119 feet wide, and almost 100 feet high. It took 8 years to complete from 1914–1922.

At its most basic level the Lincoln Memorial symbolizes the idea of Freedom. The Lincoln Memorial is often used as a gathering place for protests and political rallies. The Memorial has become a symbolically sacred venue especially for the Civil Rights movement. On August 28, 1963, the memorial grounds were the site of the *March on Washington for Jobs and Freedom*, which proved to the high point of the *American Civil Rights Movement*. It is estimated that approximately 250,000 people came to the event, where they heard Martin Luther King, Jr. deliver his historic speech *"I have a Dream."* King's speech, with its language of patriotism and its evocation of Lincoln's Gettysburg Address, was meant to match the symbolism of the Lincoln Memorial as a monument to national unity.

The Lincoln Memorial is located on the western end of the National Mall in Washington, D.C., across from the Washington Monument, and towers over the Reflecting Pool. The memorial is maintained by the U.S. National Park Service, and receives approximately 8 million visitors each year. It is open 24 hours a day and is free to all visitors.

Chapter One
EARLY BATTLES

The Battle of Bull Run (or the First Battle of Manassas) began at 5:15am on Sunday July 21, 1861, when a Union artillery piece sent a shell towards the Confederate lines. Most of the key future military leaders of the North and South were present at the battle, some in very junior positions.

The Union army, under McDowell, committed some 18,572 men and 24 guns to the fight. The Confederates, in two forces, the first

Words to Understand

Blockade: To stop people or supplies from entering or leaving a country or port, especially when at war.

Counterattack: An attack intended to stop or oppose an attack by an enemy or competitor.

Offensive: A large military attack.

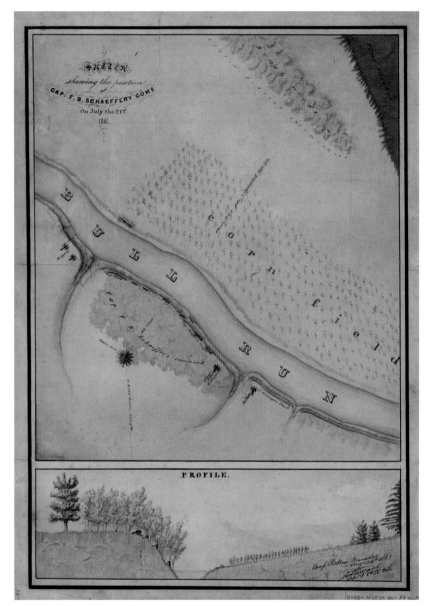

under Beauregard and the second under Joseph E. Johnston, committed 9,713 and 8,340 men respectively.

The Union force advanced, hoping to catch the Confederates unawares, but met determined opposition instead. The Confederates gave ground until they met the Virginians under Jackson. It was at Bull Run that Thomas Jackson earned his nickname "Stonewall." He adamantly refused to budge and the

OPPOSITE: The Battle of Pea Ridge, Arkansas, March 7, 1862.

ABOVE: Sheet music for the Pea Ridge March, dedicated to Major General Franz Sigel, composed by Chr. Bach. Lithograph by Kurz and Co., Milwaukee, Wisconsin.

RIGHT: The First Battle of Bull Run, a sketch showing the position of Captain F.B. Schaeffer's command along the Bull Run, 600 yards from the Lewis house on July 21, 1861.

rest of the wavering Confederate army rallied to his left and right.

It was at this point that McDowell made the error that cost him the battle. He ordered up artillery to bombard the stubborn Confederates, but faced strong batteries of Confederate artillery and got the worst of the exchange.

Suddenly, the Confederate 33rd Virginia, dressed in blue, were mistaken for Union reserves and cut down the Union artillery crews. The 33rd then charged and routed several Union regiments, while Colonel J.E.B. Stuart's cavalry seized the abandoned Union artillery. Eventually the guns were recovered and McDowell began

to feed in more troops, as did the Confederates. In the confused fight, Union troops were slipping away, back across Bull Run. Soon it turned into a rout. The Confederates had the field, seizing 5,000 muskets, half a million cartridges, 28 artillery pieces, countless horses, and masses of clothing and equipment.

The disaster cost McDowell his job and Major General George McClellan almost immediately replaced him. It was first blood to the Confederacy, the Union **blockade**

of the South having been declared but not enforced. Early attacks on the Southern coastline were working, however, the seizure of the entrance to Port Royal, South Carolina, being particularly effective in November 1861.

For both sides it appeared that the control of the Mississippi river, as far as the Gulf, was essential. The first major battle took place on August 10 at Wilson's Creek, 10 miles (16km) from Springfield. Outnumbered, the Union forces were decisively defeated.

ABOVE: View of the Bull Run river.

OPPOSITE: Virginia State Memorial, Seminary Ridge at the Gettysburg battle site.

OVERLEAF: The First Battle of Bull Run, July 21, 1861
The American School.
Lithograph published in 1889.
Collection of the New York Historical Society.

The Union army rapidly reorganized and a new offensive was mounted in February 1862. By then, the Confederates had been reinforced and had 5,000 Native Americans in support. The two armies clashed at Pea Ridge, Arkansas, between March 7 and 8, but the battle was complicated by the fact that the Native Americans scalped friend and foe alike. Despite this the Confederates were soundly beaten.

The Western Theater brought two men together who would eventually shape the war and bring military victory to the Union: Ulysses Simpson Grant and William Tecumseh Sherman.

Grant, an undistinguished West Point graduate, failed farmer, failed realtor, and failed engineer, had received his appointment as a brigadier general on August 7, 1861. Sherman, who had fought at the First Bull Run as a colonel, would join him to seize control of the Tennessee river – a vital waterway running through northern Alabama, Tennessee, and Kentucky and into Ohio. The river provided a superb opportunity to drive into the Deep South.

Firstly, the defending forts, Henry and Donelson, needed to be taken, and Grant managed to achieve this in February 1862. Grant's overwhelming victory against the Confederates brought great hope to the North. The surrender negotiations with the Confederate commander, Buckner, also gave Grant his nickname (he would earn his second later – Butcher Grant): "Yours of this date proposing

armistice and appointment of commissioner to settle terms of capitulation is received. No terms except unconditional and immediate surrender can be accepted. I propose to move immediately on your works."

Instantly, Ulysses S. Grant became Unconditional Surrender Grant, which would set the tone of his war. Grant took nearly 15,000 prisoners and he could now move steadily down the Tennessee river and take on whatever the Confederates chose to offer him.

Grant's next major battle is known either as Pittsburg Landing or Shiloh. He was peacefully eating his breakfast on the morning of April 6, 1862, when he heard heavy firing. He hastened to Pittsburg Landing, 9 miles (15km) away, to find his army under attack. His officers believed that 80,000 Confederates were assaulting their positions, but in truth there was around half this number. But this was counterbalanced by the fact that the Confederates had also overestimated Grant's army, though this had not deterred them from making a concerted attack.

The Confederate offensive consisted of three strong prongs,

ABOVE: The Battle of Bull Run, General McDowell's Union forces routed by Confederates under General Beauregard and General Joseph E. Johnston. From The New York times, July 21, 1861.

OPPOSITE LEFT: General Albert Sidney Johnson.

OPPOSITE RIGHT: General Irvin McDowell (left) with General George B. McClellan.

having the ultimate intention of driving the Union army into the Tennessee river. The Confederate left made impressive progress, but its right and center met with determined resistance, particularly around the Peach Orchard and the Hornet's Nest. As the Confederate attacks floundered, Grant was able to reorganize and hold the line until darkness fell.

The Confederates lost their able General Albert Sidney Johnston and General Beauregard took over control of the army. On the morning of April 7, Grant threw fresh reserves into the battle, while General Buell held the left and General Lew Wallis the right. As soon as Buell's **counterattack** got underway, Sherman's forces in the center moved forward, regaining the Peach Orchard and the Hornet's Nest. Beauregard's reserves were too late to help him and he decided to withdraw, taking with him 3,000 captured Union soldiers and 30 Union artillery pieces.

Total Confederate casualties amounted to 1,728 killed, 8,012 wounded, and 959 captured. The Union losses were 13,047, of which 1,754 had been killed.

Back in April 1861 the Union navy had abandoned the large dockyard facility of Gosport Navy Yard, near Portsmouth. The Confederates were delighted and captured large amounts of weapons and stores. Among the booty was the *Merrimac*, a 3,200-ton ironclad vessel, sporting 40 guns, which was renamed the *Virginia*. On March 8, 1862 the *Virginia* led an attack on Union

ABOVE: View of Port Royal, South Carolina. Photograph of the Federal navy and seaborne expeditions against the Atlantic coast of the Confederacy, 1861–62.

RIGHT: Battle of Pea Ridge, Arkansas, March 7–8, 1862
American School (19th Century). Lithograph by Kurz & Allison. Private collection.

warships on the west coast of Hampton Roads, Virginia, near Newport News, and sank several of the wooden warships. On the following day she attacked again, but this time was faced with a similar ironclad, the *Monitor*. It was the first battle ever to see ironclad warships engaged in a fight with one another, but it ended in stalemate. The *Virginia*'s end would come all too soon.

General McClellan's Union army had occupied the York Peninsula, which meant that both Norfolk and Gosport Navy Yards were vulnerable. The *Virginia* was trapped. She could not risk the open seas, nor could she risk running aground close to Union batteries. On May 10 her crew set her on fire and at 05:00am the following day she blew up. The Union *Monitor* would not last very long either. She sank at midnight on December 31, 1862, under tow into Charleston harbor.

Naval forces were an important aspect of the war. Not only did the Union navy have the job of blockading the South, it was also key in supporting army operations. By December 1863 Lincoln could report that the Union navy had a strength of 588 vessels, of which 75 were either ironclads or armored steamers.

A prime example of the importance of naval power was the struggle for the control of the Mississippi river. The Confederates were busy at work, fortifying points along the river to deny control of it to the Union. Most notable was Ship Island, which was 10 miles (16km) off

IRVIN MCDOWELL (1818–1885)

Born in Ohio, McDowell was educated in France before entering West Point, graduating in 1838. For a time he served as a tactics instructor at West Point before seeing active service during the Mexican War. At the outbreak of the American Civil War he was promoted to the rank of brigadier general, charged with protecting Washington. He singularly failed in this role, when he was decisively defeated at the First Bull Run in July 1861 and was replaced by McClellan. McDowell was eventually given command of the 1st corps of the Army of the Potomac and later served under Pope in the newly organized Army of Virginia. He was blamed for the Union failure at Second Bull Run, but was lauded and promoted for his actions at Cedar Mountain. After these two battles, however, he saw no further action and was given the post of Commander of the Pacific Coast. He was promoted to major general in 1865 and was mustered out in September the following year. He continued to serve in the regular army as a major general until his retirement in 1882, but died in San Francisco, California, three years later.

OPPOSITE: The Peach Orchard, where action during the Battle of Pittsburg Landing (Shiloh) took place in April 1862.

the coast and 60 miles (100km) from both New Orleans and Mobile. In its struggle for control of the river, the Union fixed on Ship Island as its first target, seizing control of the island in September 1861. New Orleans was an important trading port and the Confederates were building warships in the harbor. Logically, the Union needed to take the city, destroy the Confederate forts protecting the entrance to the Mississippi (St. Philip and Jackson), and then hold the waterway.

Union forces began assembling at Ship Island in February 1862, and the attack was launched the following April. Mortar ships opened fire on the two forts on April 18, firing a staggering 240 shells per hour. Despite the devastating firepower the forts held on. On April 24 the Union fleet, under Farragut, moved in closer to engage the forts' batteries. The attack worked and despite the determined Confederate defense, New Orleans fell to the Union army.

New Orleans was put under the direct rule of General Benjamin Butler, who imposed a harsh regime

ABOVE: The crew on the deck of the Monitor.

LEFT: The Battle of Wilson's Creek
Lithograph by Kurz & Allison, 1893.

OPPOSITE: *The USS* Monitor *and* Canonicus *photographed in the James river, Virginia.*

on the inhabitants of the city. Among his requirements was the surrender of all firearms. Men were required to take the Oath of Allegiance to the United States, otherwise they would have to pay a fine or be exiled. Butler would remain in post until December 24, 1862, when he returned to active service.

Meanwhile, the Peninsula Campaign had been under way since April 1862. General McClellan first moved against the Confederate-held Yorktown, defended by 15,000 men, having at his disposal upwards of 100,000 men and 44 batteries of artillery. In the first skirmish of the campaign at Lee's Mill (April 16) it was the Union that came off second best.

Facing McClellan was General Joseph E. Johnston, who proposed to abandon Yorktown and concentrate a powerful force near Richmond, which had been the strategy that had led to the abandonment of Gosport Navy Yard. McClellan sent off troops in pursuit of the retreating Confederates on May 4 and they followed the road from Yorktown to Williamsburg, clashing late that night and during the following day. It was the first of a series of inconclusive engagements.

McClellan had managed to convince himself that he was facing a force much larger than his own. He demanded reinforcements and consequently, by the end of May, his own army numbered 127,166, supported by another 14,007 men under General Wool.

On May 27 McClellan attacked a Confederate force of some 9,000 that was protecting the Virginia Central Railroad. The Union army scored a decisive victory, but to stop McClellan from seizing the initiative, the Confederates launched a counter-attack on May 31, which was beset with problems, mainly due to floodwater. The Battle of Seven Pines

ABOVE: The First Encounter of Ironclads: Terrific Engagement between the Merrimac and the Monitor, March 9, 1862
Calvert Lithographing Co., Detroit, Michigan.

LEFT: Admiral Farragut of the Union Fleet.

OPPOSITE: Ruins of Fort Moultrie in Charleston Harbor.

saw the Union corps of Keyes and Heintzelman pushed back. Men fought in water up to their knees and many of the wounded were drowned.

Another battle took place on the same day at Fair Oaks Station, in which fighting was so intense that the opposing sides resorted to bayonet attacks. The Confederates were on the verge of a great victory, but Johnston had been badly wounded and the opportunity was lost. This brought about the appointment of Robert E. Lee to take over from Johnston. Lee received reinforcements and was determined to attack McClellan and force his army away from Richmond.

First he reinforced General Jackson in the Shenandoah Valley. Jackson would be vital in his own **offensive**, and would strike at the Union right, then Lee's main force would hit Mechanicsville and fight towards Gaines' Mill. He proposed to

hit McClellan on June 26. Lee's offensive sparked off what became known as the Seven Days' Battles (June 25–July 1, 1862). On June 26 the armies clashed at Mechanicsville, on June 27 at Gaines' Mill, at Peach Orchard and Savage's Station on June 29, at Frayser's Farm (Glendale) on June 30, and at Malvern Hill on July 1.

In all, some 91,169 Union troops were engaged, of which 1,734 were killed, 8,062 wounded, and 6,053 were posted missing. Lee's Confederates amounted to some 75,769 (other accounts say 95,481), of which 3,478

ABOVE: General Benjamin F. Butler.

OPPOSITE RIGHT: Position of the Union Army on June 30, 1862, illustrating the Battle of Frayser's (Frazier's) Farm, one of the Seven Days' Battles, which began on June 26 and ended on July 1, 1862, and marked the culmination of the Peninsula Campaign.

OPPOSITE LEFT: White Oak Swamp, Henrico County, Virginia.

JAMES EWELL BROWN STUART (1833-1864)

Stuart was born in Patrick County, Virginia, the son of a lawyer and soldier who had fought in the War of 1812. Stuart graduated thirteenth in his class at West Point in 1854. He saw service in Texas during the Indian Wars and was later transferred as a cavalry officer to Fort Leavenworth. He accompanied Lee in the capture of John Brown at Harper's Ferry in 1859. Stuart was a captain by April 1861 but resigned his commission. The following month he became a lieutenant colonel in the Confederate army and was ordered to Harper's Ferry to join up with Jackson. After service in the Shenandoah Valley he fought at Bull Run in July 1861, and two months later was promoted to brigadier general, fighting the Battles of Yorktown and Williamsburg in the Peninsula. As a consummate cavalry commander he was invaluable to Lee during the Seven Days' Battles and at Second Bull Run in August 1862. After the battles of Antietam and Fredericksburg he took over Stonewall Jackson's corps, and in June 1863 fought the inconclusive battle at Brandy Station. He was criticized for not arriving until the second day of the Battle of Gettysburg. During the Wilderness Campaign of 1864 he stopped Union troops at Yellow Tavern, en route to Richmond, but was wounded and died on May 12, 1864. Lee missed him greatly for his constant protection from unexpected attacks by the Union forces.

were killed, 16,261 were wounded, and 875 were posted missing.

Despite the casualties, it was McClellan who was in retreat, heading for Harrison's Landing, near the James river, his campaign in the Peninsula now at an end, having lost 15,249 dead, wounded or missing. The Confederates had taken over 10,000 prisoners, captured 52 guns, and 35,000 muskets and pistols.

General Pope assumed command of a new force called the Army of Virginia on June 26, 1862, his Union army first pushing towards Gordonsville. Lee, meanwhile, confident that McClellan's army held no threat, had despatched Jackson and Ewell to Gordonsville on July 13, with Pope becoming aware of the Confederate movement on August 8. Late the next day Union troops moved to within 2 miles (3km) of Cedar Mountain (Slaughter Mountain), where they were engaged by the forward elements of the Confederate army. The outnumbered Union troops first pushed forward, but were then checked and pushed back. Total Union losses amounted to nearly 2,500, whereas the

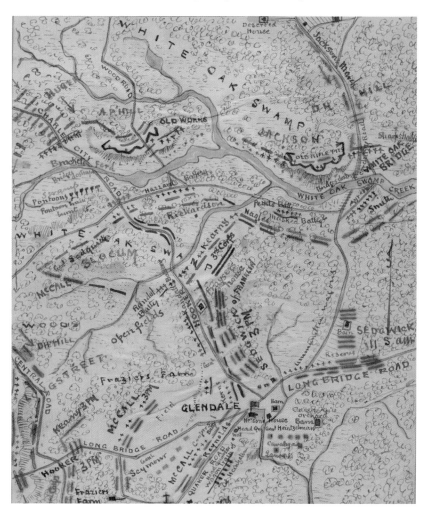

Confederates lost 1,300 men.

With more Union forces arriving, the Confederates fell back across the Rapidan river. Lee was planning another offensive, but Union cavalry captured his orders on August 16. Pope knew he could not count on McClellan's help and that the full force of Lee's army would soon strike his own men. Lee pressed on with his audacious attack. Jackson, supported by Stuart's cavalry, covered 51 miles (82km) in two days to reach Bristoe Station on August 27. Jackson aimed to capture the considerable

amount of Union stores held at Manassas Junction.

After a series of skirmishes, Pope abandoned his defensive line and on the same day headed for Manassas Junction, by way of Gainesville, while part of his army clashed with Ewell at Kettle Run, near Bristoe Station. Pope determined to concentrate his army at Manassas Junction and then destroy Jackson before Ewell could support him. Meanwhile, Lee was following the same route Jackson had taken and was closing in on Pope.

The Second Battle of Bull Run (or Manassas) got underway on Friday August 29, 1862. Fighting was severe but by the end of the first day Pope thought he had beaten Lee. Pope reported losses of 8,000 and told Washington that Lee had lost twice that number and was in full retreat. He was wrong. Lee attacked the next day and Pope's weary men withdrew. Union losses amounted to 14,462, while the Confederates lost 9,474 men. Pope had missed a golden opportunity to destroy Lee and was forced to resign.

McClellan, despite everything, once again took control of the Union army. He knew that Lee would aim for

ABOVE: The Battle of Seven Pines (Battle of Fair Oaks), fought from May 31–June 1, 1862, was part of the Peninsula Campaign. A 32–pdr. field howitzer is pictured in the foreground.

OPPOSITE ABOVE: The Fair Oaks battle site.

OPPOSITE BELOW LEFT: General John Ellis Wool.

OPPOSITE BELOW RIGHT: Fair Oaks, Virginia. The old frame house on the battle site was used by Hooker's division as a hospital.

Research Projects

List chronologically and summarize the principle battles of the Civil War.

Maryland and Pennsylvania now that the Peninsula was free of Union troops and Richmond was no longer under threat. On September 8 Lee issued a proclamation to Maryland, begging it to join the Confederacy and promising that his army would come and protect the state. The Confederate army began to move on September 12. The following day Lee learned that a large Union army was at South Mountain; this was a matter of

BELOW: Savage's Station served as a Union field hospital after the battle of June 29, 1862.

OPPOSITE: The ruins of Gaines' Mill, in the vicinity of Cold Harbor, during the Peninsula Campaign, fought between April and July 1862, in which the Union failed to capture Richmond, Virginia.

OVERLEAF: Battle of Williamsburg, 5 May 1862
American School (19th Century). Lithograph by Kurz & Allison.

concern, for at this point his army was split into three moving columns.

Jackson had headed for Harper's Ferry, which he seized, taking 12,000 prisoners, while Longstreet was at Hagerstown and Hill was 13 miles (21km) away at Boonsboro'. Lee had not counted on McClellan moving to stop him, but the Union general had come into possession of one of Lee's orders, showing the routes that would be taken by his troops. McClellan took the order at face value and realized he had a chance to destroy the Confederate army piecemeal.

Text-Dependent Questions

1. What is the alternative name given to the Battle of Bull Run?

2. When did the Battle of Bull Run commence?

3. Why was Thomas Jackson nicknamed "Stonewall?"

Chapter Two
THE FIGHTING CONTINUES

On September 14 Union troops tried to force the passes around South Mountain, but met with mixed results. Around 28,000 Union troops were involved, facing 18,000 Confederates. By 8:00pm Lee was convinced his plan was compromised and that the army should retreat to Sharpsburg before proceeding across the Potomac river. There were simply too many risks in trying to remain on the offensive.

Union troops marched through South Mountain, across the valley,

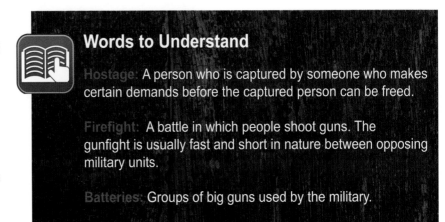

Words to Understand

Hostage: A person who is captured by someone who makes certain demands before the captured person can be freed.

Firefight: A battle in which people shoot guns. The gunfight is usually fast and short in nature between opposing military units.

Batteries: Groups of big guns used by the military.

OPPOSITE: Cedar Mountain (Slaughter's Mountain), the site of the battle of August 9, 1862. A Confederate battery was sited near Parson Slaughter's house in 1862.

ABOVE: Pontoon bridge across the James river.

and took up positions on the high ground near Antietam Creek. This was a stream with a number of fords and three stone-arched bridges. Lee proposed to make a determined stand at Sharpsburg, just to the west of Antietam Creek.

McClellan had 87,000 men and Lee 59,000, though only 55,000 and 40,000 respectively were engaged. The extremely costly Battle of Antietam got underway on September 17, with artillery opening fire at dawn; the

Union army launched the first assault, with waves of infantry advancing towards the Confederate lines.

One of the most dramatic features of the battle was the crossing of a stone bridge, later dubbed Burnside's Bridge. General Burnside's Union troops tried to force the bridge three times, the assaults taking place between 10:00am and 1:00pm, when he eventually succeeded. The assaults cost one of Burnside's brigades along with some 463 casualties.

By nightfall both sides were exhausted. The heavy losses, around 11,500 for each army, blunted Lee's plans, but McClellan failed to follow up and was content to concentrate on reorganizing his forces.

Frustrated by the lack of action, Lincoln demanded that McClellan cross the Potomac river and drive Lee south. McClellan still held back, missing the chance to intercept Lee en route to Richmond. Lee had not been idle; he ordered J.E.B. Stuart, his cavalry commander, to raid Pennsylvania. Stuart started out on October 9 and despite being pursued was able to capture 1,200 horses and take 30 **hostages** before returning to Virginia.

Burnside assumed control of the Army of the Potomac on November 7, 1862 – once again McClellan had been

ABOVE: Burnside's Bridge was the controversial means by which General Ambrose Burnside and his troops crossed Antietam Creek during the Battle of Antietam.

OPPOSITE: A signal station on Elk Mountain, overlooking the battlefield of Antietam, during the Maryland Campaign.

LEFT: The Battle of Antietam, 1862
American School (19th Century).
Lithograph by Kurz & Allison.
Private collection.

replaced. Burnside was a reluctant commander, a strict disciplinarian and a difficult man to please. After yet another reorganization his army started towards Fredericksburg, reaching Falmouth, near Fredericksburg, on November 17. Lee and his army, meanwhile, reached the heights around Fredericksburg two days later.

Burnside dithered for 20 days, giving Lee the opportunity to dig in and site his artillery ready for an attack. At 03:00am on December 11 Confederate signal guns gave warning that the Union army was on the move. Burnside concentrated his artillery on Fredericksburg itself and Union infantry was used to storm the town. After Fredericksburg fell there was a lull in the fighting until the morning of December 13, when Union troops assaulted the Confederate line, only to be beaten back by the timely arrival of reinforcements. The leading Union regiments lost around 40 percent of their strength.

Burnside was unable to dislodge the Confederates, however much he tried. He had 113,000 men, but at Fredericksburg he had lost 12,500. Lee's Confederates amounted to 72,497 directly engaged and they had suffered losses of 5,322. Burnside desperately wanted to attack again, but needed to regroup. It took him until January 20, 1863 to be ready, but by then heavy rains and mud impeded his chances of forcing a battle. Lincoln had seen enough and replaced Burnside with Joseph Hooker.

OPPOSITE: Ruins of the railroad bridge at Blackburn's Ford, Bull Run.

JACKSON, THOMAS JONATHAN "STONEWALL" (1824–1863)

Jackson was born at Clarksburg, West Virginia, and was only two when his father died of typhoid. Jackson entered West Point in 1842, graduating seventeenth out of fifty-nine in 1846. He served in the Mexican War, receiving commendations and promotions for his gallantry, and ended the war as a major. Jackson resigned from the army in 1851 to teach at the Virginia Military Institute in Lexington. In 1859 he was the academy's representative at the execution of the abolitionist, John Brown, where he stood guard. In June 1861 Jackson became a brigadier general in the Confederate army, taking command of the Confederates in the Shenandoah Valley the following October. During the summer of 1862 he won several victories against the Union army before joining Lee in East Virginia. With Lee, he fought in the Seven Days' Battles, and at the Battles of Cedar Mountain, Second Bull Run, and Antietam. In October 1862 he became a lieutenant general and was now in command of half the Army of Northern Virginia. He wintered at Chancellorsville and was unfortunately shot by one of his own troops on the evening of May 2, 1863, which led to his arm being amputated. Unfortunately, he developed pneumonia and died on May 10. Lee said of him "... he has lost his left arm; but I have lost my right arm."

ABOVE: Soldiers photographed during the Second Battle of Bull Run (Second Battle of Manassas), August 29–30, 1862.

LEFT: Manassas Junction: damaged rolling stock belonging to the Orange & Alexandria Railroad.

OPPOSITE: The remains of a house after battle, Bull Run.

"Fighting Joe" Hooker took control of the Army of the Potomac on January 25, 1863. He realized that one of the main problems so far was that the Union army had never managed to use its manpower advantage and that only parts of the army had fought in each engagement. On paper, Hooker had 130,000 men, and Lee had barely half that number.

Hooker determined not to attack Lee's defensive positions but to outmaneuver him. He left a covering force and marched the bulk of his army along the Rappahannock river, crossing it to place himself behind the Confederate line. Hooker sent his cavalry, under Stoneman, to cut off Lee's supply lines to Richmond. Stoneman began his raid on April 29,

1863. Meanwhile the main Union army was around Chancellorsville.

On the following day Hooker pushed his men up the Orange Turnpike from Chancellorsville to Fredericksburg, meeting with determined resistance. With his lead elements in retreat, Hooker set up defensive positions around Chancellorsville. Meanwhile,

ABOVE: Antietam Creek, Maryland.

LEFT: Monument to the Battles of Bull Run.

OPPOSITE ABOVE: Harper's Ferry, with a view of the town and railroad bridge, 1862. The town lies where the Potomac and Shenandoah rivers meet.

OPPOSITE BELOW: Many old Civil War forts and campsites can be found on Maryland Heights, Harper's Ferry.

Confederate cavalry commander J.E.B. Stuart discovered that Hooker's right flank was unprotected and Lee immediately ordered Stonewall Jackson to lead his 28,000-man corps to attack it.

Jackson's troops collided with the Union General Howard's corps at Dowdall's Tavern. It was now the afternoon of May 2, 1863. Emerging from the woodland tracks the Confederates swept towards Howard's 11th Corps. After an initial **firefight**, which had caught the Union troops unprepared, many of the Union soldiers fled and only darkness saved Howard's men from complete

annihilation. At around 9:00pm, riding to scout the positions of the enemy, Jackson was accidentally shot by some of his own men. He failed to recover from his wounds and died on May 10.

By now, Lee realized that the Union forces facing his defensive lines near Fredericksburg were depleted, and he could afford to send more troops to attack Hooker. Around 10,000 Confederates were left to man Marye's Heights. The covering Union force attacked under General Sedgwick, who had 23,000 men at his disposal. Sedgwick's men took

ABOVE: General Burnside and his Staff, at Warrenton, Virginia.

OPPOSITE: Sudley Ford, Bull Run.

severe casualties but the Confederate line was turned and the rebel defenders fell back.

On May 4 a determined Confederate counter-attack pushed Sedgwick off Marye's Heights.

Sedgwick then received an order from Hooker to pull back, but at 9.15am Hooker was wounded at Chancellor House. His orders to his subordinates were to withdraw and to protect Washington.

Union losses were around 16,000, around a quarter of them now prisoners, while Confederate losses were around 12,827. Now Hooker had missed a great chance; he had been indecisive and, had he reinforced

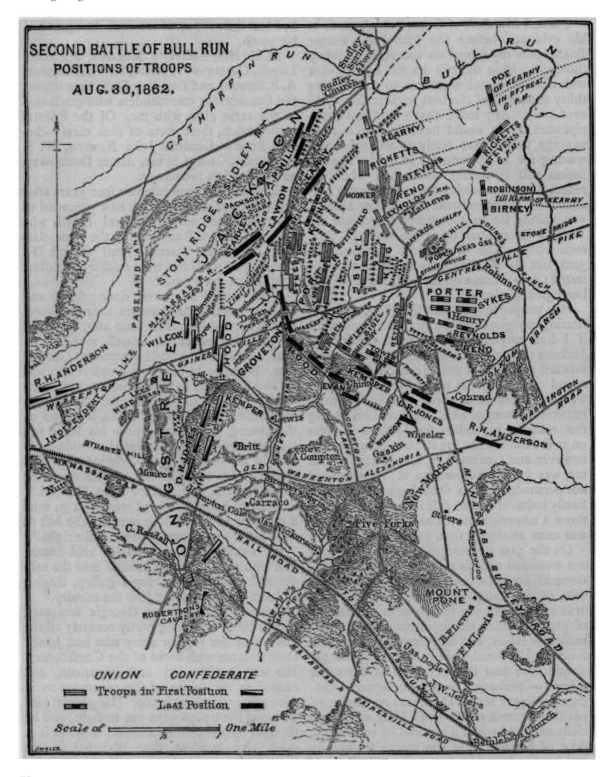

SECOND BATTLE OF BULL RUN
POSITIONS OF TROOPS
AUG. 30, 1862.

Howard when Jackson first attacked, he would have rolled up the Confederate army.

By mid-May 1862 General Henry Halleck had combined the Armies of the Mississippi, Ohio, and Tennessee and was pushing towards Corinth. Facing him were Beauregard's 50,000

Confederates, while Halleck could muster 100,000 men.

Memphis had fallen to the Union in July 1862. It was now possible to navigate as far as Confederate-held Vicksburg, but in September 1862 the

Confederates had seized Ruka, Mississippi, and in early October had attacked Corinth.

Grant proposed to move on Vicksburg, but it would be a tough assignment. The United States Navy

OPPOSITE: Map showing the positions of troops, roads, railroads, towns, rivers, houses, names of residents, etc., on August 30, 1862, at the end of the Second Battle of Bull Run.

ABOVE: Catharpin Run, Sudley Church, and the remains of the Sudley Sulphur Spring, Bull Run.

RIGHT: Soldiers relaxing at Brandy Station, Virginia. The Battle of Brandy Station was fought on June 9, 1863, at the start of the Gettysburg Campaign. Bull Run.

commander, Farragut, had first called on Vicksburg to surrender in May 1862. He could not press his point, however, because he was not strong enough to duel with the **batteries** defending the city. Grant now proposed to disembark his army just below Vicksburg, covered by the navy. Consequently, on April 16, 1863 the navy started out and began to engage the Confederate batteries that night. Meanwhile, Grant's troops landed ready for an assault on the city. Elements of Grant's force, under Sherman, marched cross-country and attacked Confederate towns as far as Jackson on the Pearl river. Grant's men slowly advanced on Vicksburg, expecting a major fight to wrest the city from the Confederacy.

OPPOSITE ABOVE: Fortifications outside Fredericksburg.

OPPOSITE BELOW: The North Anna bridge after it had been destroyed, Fredericksburg.

ABOVE: Ruins of a house at Chancellorsville.

RIGHT: The Rappahannock river and Germanna Ford.

RIGHT: Map of the Battle of Chancellorsville.

BELOW: Major General Henry W. Halleck.

OVERLEAF: The Battle of Chancellorsville, Virginia, April 30– May 6, 1863
Lithograph by Kurz & Allison.

Facing Grant was General Pemberton, who by July 1 realized that unless he got help very soon, Vicksburg was doomed. Lee could not afford to detach men from his army and consequently a white flag was raised over Vicksburg on July 3. The following day Pemberton's garrison of 30,000 men surrendered.

By July 9 Grant was at Jackson, chasing General Johnston's army of

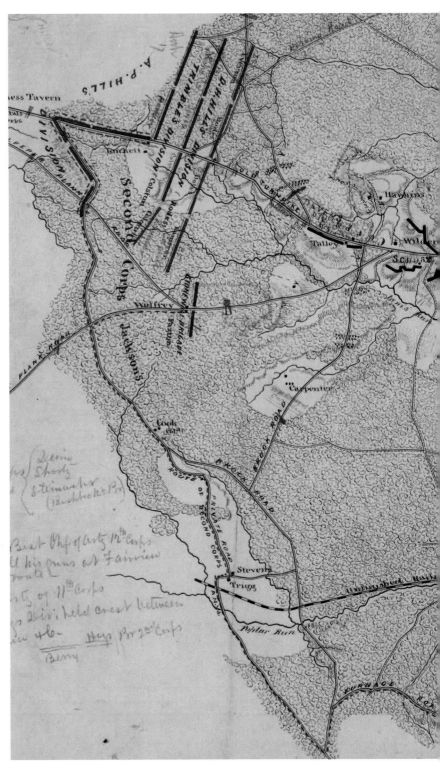

Map of the
Battle of Chancellorsville,
Saturday, May 2nd 1863.

Scale 2 inches to One mile

22,000 men. Johnston was determined not to yield any further ground. He repulsed a Union attack on 12 July, but withdrew four days later.

That same day Port Hudson, Louisiana, some 135 miles (217km) upriver from New Orleans, fell to Union forces. It had had a large garrison but this had been stripped to support Vicksburg. Facing the 7,000 defenders were 20,000 Union troops under General Banks. After a stiff fight the Confederates surrendered and 6,000 prisoners were taken. This is of great significance to African-Americans as it was the first battle to see black troops of the Corps D'Afrique within the Union ranks.

Back in Virginia in the spring of 1863 Lee had been charged with the task of bringing the war to the North. He was confident that Richmond was not under threat and proposed to

JOSEPH HOOKER (1814–1879)

Hooker was born in Massachusetts and graduated from West Point before serving in the Seminole and Mexican Wars. He became involved in fierce disputes with General Winfield Scott, which led him to resign from the army, and he was not recalled until August 1861. He was a heavy drinker and was disagreeable and aggressive, which earned him his nickname "Fighting Joe." Hooker was promoted to the rank of major general and fought at the Battle of Seven Pines and in the Seven Days' Battles, and served under Pope at the Second Bull Run, Antietam and Fredericksburg. He became commander of the Army of the Potomac, relieving Burnside of the position, but lost his first battle at Chancellorsville and was replaced by Meade. From then on Hooker served in support roles, but took Lookout Mountain and Missionary Ridge. He was mustered out in 1866 but two years later suffered a stroke. Hooker's name is forever linked with the nickname given to the prostitutes that followed his army and he is often described as having been immodest and immoral. He died in Long Island, New York, in October 1879 and was buried in Cincinnati.

OPPOSITE: Wounded Indian sharpshooters on Marye's Heights.

BELOW: The Siege of Vicksburg, 1863
Lithograph by Kurz & Allison, 1888

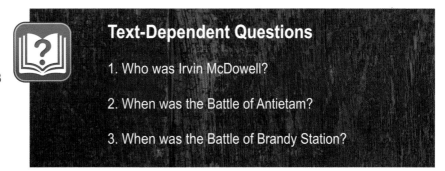

Text-Dependent Questions

1. Who was Irvin McDowell?

2. When was the Battle of Antietam?

3. When was the Battle of Brandy Station?

strike deep into Pennsylvania. After reorganizing the Army of Northern Virginia he set out, leaving a shadow force to watch Hooker's army. By early June there were scattered reports of large columns of Confederate infantry in the Shenandoah Valley, heading north.

On June 28, 1863 the Army of the Potomac had yet another commander, when General George Meade, who faced a baptism of fire, replaced Hooker. He needed to reorganize, then find Lee and beat him. The Confederates had learned that the Army of the Potomac was on the move, and Lee was concerned that the Union army would get behind him and cut him off. He ordered his troops to concentrate around Carlisle and Gettysburg.

Chapter Three
THE BATTLE OF GETTYSBURG

Early on the morning of July 1, Lee rode from his headquarters at Greenwood, along the Chambersburg Pike, towards Gettysburg. He had barely begun his ride when he heard artillery fire. Running north-east from Gettysburg was the road to Philadelphia, to the north Carlisle was 27 miles (43km) away, while to the south-west the road ran to Hagerstown, barely 6 miles (10km) distant.

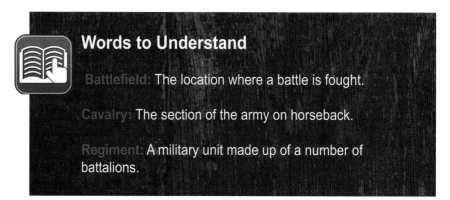

Words to Understand

Battlefield: The location where a battle is fought.

Cavalry: The section of the army on horseback.

Regiment: A military unit made up of a number of battalions.

Meade had given control of three corps of infantry and **cavalry** to General John Reynolds, who was certain that a battle was imminent and had taken up position on the Emmitsburg Road, close to Marsh Creek. He had cavalry watching Gettysburg under Buford.

The first Confederate troops appeared early on July 1, approaching Gettysburg, but dismounted Union cavalry held them off. Reynolds and Buford quickly realized the seriousness of the situation and Reynolds ordered his corps to march on Gettysburg. Both sides poured men into the battle and by mid-afternoon

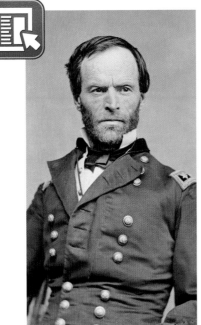

WILLIAM TECUMSEH SHERMAN (1820–1891)

Sherman was born at Lancaster, Ohio, in 1820, but his father, a lawyer, died when his son was only nine. He attended West Point military academy, where he graduated sixth in 1840. He was later regarded as something of an eccentric, but he was a tenacious fighter and ruthless leader, especially in the latter stages of the American Civil War. He was at the First Battle of Bull Run in 1861, where he commanded a brigade of volunteers, after which he was

promoted to brigadier general and sent to Kentucky as deputy commander of the Department of the Cumberland, under Robert Anderson, the hero of Fort Sumter, whom he later succeeded. He served under General Ulysses S. Grant in 1862 and 1863 during the campaigns that led to the fall of the Confederate stronghold of Vicksburg on the Mississippi river, and which culminated in the defeat of the Confederate armies in the state of Tennessee. In 1864, Sherman succeeded Grant as Union commander in the Western Theater of war. He proceeded to capture the city of Atlanta, a military success that contributed decisively to the re-election of Abraham Lincoln as president. Sherman's famous "'March to the Sea," through Georgia and the Carolinas, further undermined the Confederates, and he accepted the surrender of all the Confederate armies in the Carolinas, Georgia, and Florida in April 1865. After the civil war, Sherman replaced Grant as Commanding General of the Army (1869–83), and as such, was responsible for the conduct of the Indian Wars in the Western United States. He steadfastly refused to be drawn into politics and in 1875 published his memoirs, one of the most vivid accounts of the American Civil War. He retired in February 1884 and died in New York in 1891.

LEFT: Battery B, Second U.S. Artillery.

the Union forces had fallen back to a defensive line along Cemetery Hill. With more troops arriving, darkness fell, and it was necessary to postpone the engagement until morning.

The second day of the battle centered on geographical features that have come to mean much in American history. The extreme left flank of the Union army rested on Big Round Top, Little Round Top, and the Devil's Den, and it was here that the main weight of the Confederate attack took place on July 2. Overshadowed by the gallant heroics of the **battlefield** in this area, there were also other major fights that day, particularly the Confederate assaults on the right flank of the Union army at Culp's Hill. In each case, determined Union defenders met equally determined Confederate assaults.

It was the third day of Gettysburg, July 3, that lived most vividly in the memory of those who fought in the battle and which captured the imagination of generations thereafter. With Lee rebuffed on the previous day, uncharacteristically he resorted to desperate measures to dislodge the Union army from its defensive positions. General Pickett's three brigades had arrived during the afternoon of July 2, and his men would lead an attack on the Union center, supported by attacks on the Union right.

Pickett's 12,500 men (of his total of 15,000), after a two-hour bombardment, charged out of the woods of Seminary Ridge, straight at the area of the Union line in front of Meade's headquarters. Beneath a torrent of fire the Confederates pressed on, the Confederate batteries being unable to assist for fear of hitting their own men. Leading Confederate **regiments** lost between 50 to 70 percent of their strength as they ran straight into musket volleys and grapeshot. For brief moments the Confederates overran Union artillery batteries, but fresh waves of Union reinforcements beat them back. Some surrendered, others ran back, but the dead and the wounded were predominant in the field.

Lee rode back to console Pickett and his men. It had been a gallant

OPPOSITE ABOVE: Three Confederate prisoners, Gettysburg, Pennsylvania.

OPPOSITE BELOW: Headquarters of General Lee on the Chambersburg Pike, Gettysburg.

ABOVE: Big Round Top, Gettysburg.

Research Projects

Summarize the events during the Battle of Gettysburg. Who where the generals? How many soldiers were engaged? What was the outcome?

GEORGE BRINTON MCCLELLAN (1826–1885)

McClellan was born in Philadelphia, Pennsylvania. He graduated from West Point in 1846, where he was second in his class. He served as an engineering officer during the Mexican War, and between 1848 and 1851 taught military engineering at West Point, later becoming Chief Engineer of the Department of Texas. In March 1855 he was assigned to the cavalry, where he developed the famous McClellan Saddle. From 1857 to 1861 he worked as a civilian, having resigned his commission, but he joined the Ohio Volunteers and was given the command of the Department of Ohio. McClellan then took command of the Army of the Potomac but, partly due to illness and dithering, made little progress and was replaced in March 1862. After Pope was defeated at the Second Bull Run in August 1862, McClellan was given command once again, leading his men at South Mountain and at Antietam, but lost command once again in November 1862. He was told to return to New Jersey to await orders, which never came. McClellan stood against Lincoln in the presidential election of 1864 and having failed to beat Lincoln, became New Jersey's governor in the 1870s and 1880s. He died in October 1885 at Orange, New Jersey.

men and had taken 20,451 casualties.

In November 1863 Lincoln visited the battlefield and delivered his famous Gettysburg address: "The world will little note, nor long remember, what we say here, but it can never forget what they did here. It is for us the living, rather, to be dedicated here to the unfinished work which they who fought here have thus far so nobly advanced. It is rather for us to be here dedicated to the great task remaining before us – that from these honored dead we take increased devotion to that cause for which they gave their last full measure of devotion."

Gettysburg saw the last major Confederate attempt to invade the

BELOW: Men gathered at Gettysburg for the laying of the cornerstone of the Soldier's National Monument, on the anniversary of Gettysburg in 1865.

OPPOSITE: The Field of Gettysburg, July 1–3, 1863
Theodore Ditterline.
Lithograph. Duval & Son 1863.

attempt, but in truth Lee realized he had made a serious error of judgement. Pickett told him "I have no division now."

Lee took full responsibility for the failure. However, the Union army was in no better shape and could not advance; but Lee and the Army of Northern Virginia had been bested and heavy casualties had been inflicted on the Confederates.

Meade had had 93,500 men engaged in the battle and had lost a staggering 23,003, and Confederate losses were proportionately more grievous. Lee had deployed 75,054

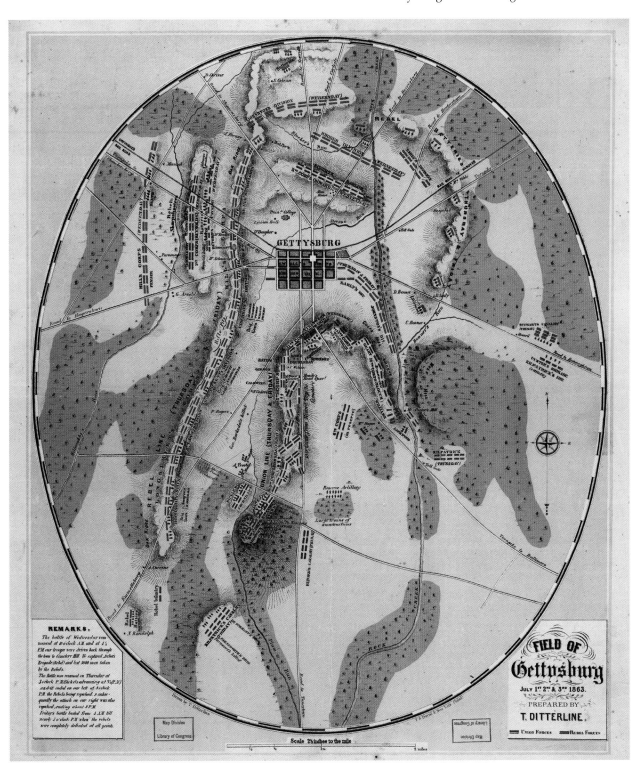

North. Again, the Union army could have finished the war had Meade struck against Lee's crippled army. The Army of the Potomac had suffered defeats at the hands of the Confederates too often, and ditherers had commanded them for too long; now they hoped to enjoy the fruits of a great victory.

Coupled with the loss of Vicksburg, the Battle of Gettysburg saw the high tide of the Confederate

Text-Dependent Questions

1. Where was General Lee's headquarters?

2. When and where did Lincoln deliver the Gettysburg address?

3. Why was the Battle of Gettysburg the Confederate's last attempt to invade the north?

BELOW: The Battle of Gettysburg, the charge of the Confederates on Cemetery Ridge, July 2, 1863

RIGHT: Map of the Battle of Gettysburg, showing troop and military positions.

successes ebb and flow away. From now on the war would be fought on the Union's terms.

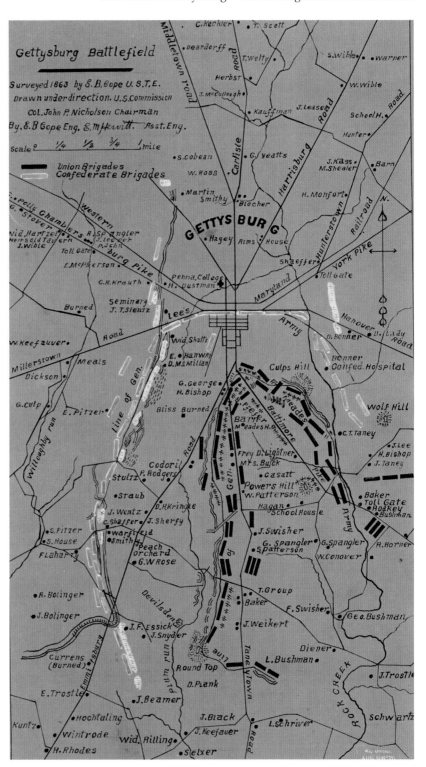

TIME LINE OF THE CIVIL WAR

1860

November 6
Abraham Lincoln elected president.

December 20
South Carolina secedes from the Union, followed two months later by other states.

1861

February 9
Jefferson Davis becomes the first and only President of the Confederate States of America.

March 4
Lincoln sworn in as 16th President of the United States.

April 12
Confederates, under Beauregard, open fire on Fort Sumter at Charleston, South Carolina.

April 15
Lincoln issues a proclamation calling for 75,000 volunteers.

April 17
Virginia secedes from the Union, followed by three other states, making an 11-state Confederacy.

April 19
Blockade proclamation issued by Lincoln.

April 20
Robert E. Lee resigns his command in the United States Army.

July 4
Congress authorizes a call for half a million volunteers.

July 21
Union forces, under McDowell, defeated at Bull Run.

July 27
McClellan replaces McDowell.

November 1
McClellan becomes general-in-chief of Union forces after the resignation of Winfield Scott.

November 8
Two Confederate officials are seized en route to Great Britain by the Union navy.

1862

February 6
Grant captures Fort Henry in Tennessee.

March 8–9
The Confederate ironclad *Merrimac* sinks two Union warships, then fights the *Monitor*.

April 6–7
Confederates attack Grant at Shiloh on the Tennessee river.

April 24
Union ships under Farragut take New Orleans.

May 31
Battle of Seven Pines, where Joseph E. Johnston is badly wounded when he nearly defeats McClellan's army.

June 1
Robert E. Lee takes over from Johnston and renames the force the Army of Northern Virginia.

June 25–July 1
Lee attacks McClellan near Richmond during the Seven Days' Battles. McClellan retreats towards Washington.

July 11
Henry Halleck becomes general -in-chief of the Union army.

August 29–30
Union army, under Pope, defeated by Jackson and Longstreet at the Second Battle of Bull Run.

September 4–9
Lee invades the North, pursued by McClellan's Union army.

September 17
Battle of Antietam. Both sides are badly mauled. Lee withdraws to Virginia.

September 22
Preliminary Emancipation Proclamation issued by Lincoln.

November 7
McClellan replaced by Burnside as commander of the Army of the Potomac.

December 13
Burnside decisively defeated at Fredericksburg, Virginia, 1863.

1863
January 1
Lincoln issues the final Emancipation Proclamation.

January 29
Grant assumes command of the Army of the West.

March 3
U.S. Congress authorizes conscription.

May 1–4
Hooker is decisively defeated by Lee at the Battle of Chancellorsville. Stonewall Jackson is mortally wounded.

June 3
Lee invades the North, heading into Pennsylvania.

June 28
George Meade replaces Hooker as commander of the Army of the Potomac.

July 1–3
Lee is defeated at the Battle of Gettysburg.

July 4
Vicksburg – the last

Confederate stronghold on the Mississippi – falls to Grant and the Confederacy is now split in two.

July 13–16
Draft riots in New York

July 18
54th Massachusetts, under Shaw, fails in its assault against Fort Wagner, South Carolina.

August 21
Quantrill's raiders murder the inhabitants of Lawrence, Kansas

September 19–20
Bragg's Confederate Army of Tennessee defeats General Rosecrans at Chickamauga.

October 16
Grant given command of all operations in the West.

November 19
Lincoln gives his famous Gettysburg Address.

November 23–25
Grant defeats Bragg at Chattanooga.

1864
March 9
Grant assumes command of all armies of the Union. Sherman takes Grant's old job as commander in the West.

May 5–6
Battle of the Wilderness.

May 8–12
Battle of Spotsylvania.

June 1–3
Battle of Cold Harbor.

June 15
Union troops miss a chance to capture Petersburg.

July 20
Sherman defeats Hood at Atlanta.

August 29
Former General McClellan becomes the Democratic nominee for president.

September 2
Atlanta is captured by Sherman.

October 19
Sheridan defeats Early's Confederates in the Shenandoah Valley.

November 8
Lincoln is re-elected president.

November 15
Sherman begins his March to the Sea.

December 15–16
Hood is defeated at the Battle of Nashville.

December 21 Sherman reached Savannah in Georgia.

1865
January 31
Thirteenth amendment approved to abolish slavery.

February 3
Peace conference between Lincoln and Confederate vice president fails at Hampton Roads, Virginia.

March 4
Lincoln inaugurated as president.

March 25
Lee's last offensive is defeated after four hours at Petersburg

April 2
Grant pushes through Lee's defensive lines at Petersburg. Richmond is evacuated as Union troops enter.

April 4
Lincoln tours Richmond.

April 9
Lee surrenders his army to Grant at Appomattox Courthouse, Virginia.

April 10
Major victory celebrations in Washington.

April 14
Lincoln shot in a Washington theater.

April 15
Lincoln dies and Andrew Johnson becomes president.

April 18
Confederate General Johnston surrenders to Sherman in North Carolina.

April 19
Lincoln's funeral procession.

April 26
Lincoln's assassin, Booth, is shot and dies in Virginia

May 23–24
Victory parade held in Washington

December 6
Thirteenth Amendment approved by Congress. It is ratified and slavery is formally abolished

BELOW: Statue of Thomas "Stonewall" Jackson at Gettysburg National Military Park.

Educational Videos about the American Civil War

The Gettysburg Address
A speech by U.S. President Abraham Lincoln, one of the best-known in American history. It was delivered by Lincoln during the American Civil War, on the afternoon of Thursday, November 19, 1863, at the dedication of the Soldiers' National Cemetery in Gettysburg, Pennsylvania.

Everyday Animated Map
A useful video explaining how the Union and Confederate armies gained ground through the various battles.

"Dear Sarah," A Soldier's Farewell to his Wife
A Civil War soldier's heartbreaking farewell letter written before his death at Bull Run.

The War Between the States
Historian Garry Adleman gives an overview of the causes, campaigns, and conclusion of the Civil War.

History, Key Figures, and Battles
A useful, concise dramatized, video explaining the American Civil War.

EXAMPLES OF CONFEDERATE UNIFORMS

Robert E. Lee in his general's uniform

Trooper, Stuart's Cavalry Corps.

Infantry Soldier

Marines

Virginia Cavalry

Louisiana
Tigers

Georgia
Infantry

4th Alabama
Regiment

South
Carolina
Regiment

Engineer

73

EXAMPLES OF UNION (FEDERAL) UNIFORMS

Ulysses S. Grant in his general's uniform

Indiana Regiment

5th New York Volunteers

39th New York Voluntry Infantry Regiment

Iron Brigade of the U.S.

U.S. Marine Corps

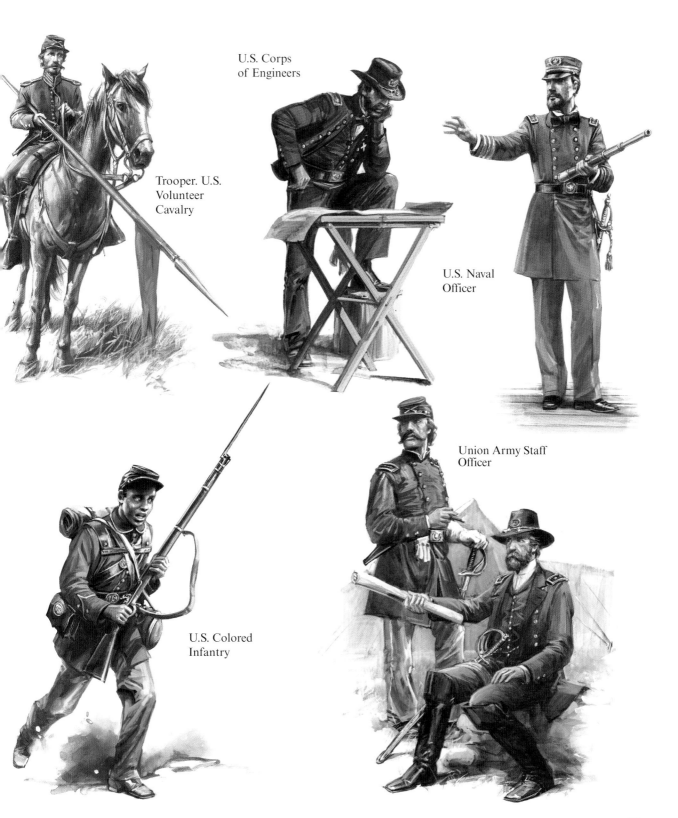

Trooper. U.S.
Volunteer
Cavalry

U.S. Corps
of Engineers

U.S. Naval
Officer

U.S. Colored
Infantry

Union Army Staff
Officer

Series Glossary of Key Terms

Abolitionist A person who wants to eliminate slavery.

Antebellum A term describing the United States before the Civil War.

Artillery Large bore firearms like cannons and mortars.

Assassination A murder for political reasons (usually an important person).

Cash Crop A crop such as cotton, sugar cane, or tobacco sold for cash.

Cavalry A section of the military mounted on horseback.

Confederacy Also called the South or the Confederate States of America. A term given to 11 southern states seceding from the United States in 1860 and 1861.

Copperhead A person in the North who sympathized with the South during the Civil war.

Dixie A nickname given to states in the south-east United States.

Dred Scott Decision A decision made by the Supreme Court that said Congress could not outlaw slavery.

Emancipation An act of setting someone free from slavery.

Gabion A basket filled with rocks and earth used to build fortifications.

Fugitive Slave Law A law passed by Congress in 1850 that stipulated escaped slaves in free states had to be retured to their owners.

Infantry Soldiers that travel and fight on foot.

North The states located in the north of the United States, also called the Union.

Plantation An area of land especially in hot parts of the world where crops such as cotton and tobacco are grown.

Slavery The state of a person who is owned or under the control of another.

Secession Withdrawal from the Federal goverment of the United States.

Sectionalism A tendency to be concerned with local interests and customs ahead of the larger country.

South The states located in the south of the United States, also called the Confederacy.

Union The name given to the states that stayed loyal to the United States.

West Point The United States Military Academy.

Yankee A nickname given for people from the North and Union soldiers.

Further Reading and Internet Resources

WEBSITES
http://www.civilwar.org

http://www.historyplace.com/civilwar

http://www.historynet.com/civil-war

www.britannica.com/event/American-Civil-War

BOOKS

Bruce Catton. *The Centennial History of the Civil War,* Doubleday, 1962. Kindle edition 2013.

Ulysses S. Grant. *The Complete Personal Memoirs of Ulysses S.* Grant Seven Treasures Publications, 2009

James Robertson and Neil Kagan. *The Untold Civil War: Exploring the Human Side of War*. National Geographic, 2011.

If you enjoyed this book take a look at Mason Crest's other war series:

The Vietnam War, World War II, Major U.S. Historical Wars.

Index

In this book, page numbers in **bold italic font** indicate photos or videos.

33rd Virginia, 13

PHOTOGRAPHIC ACKNOWLEDGEMENTS
All images in this book are supplied by the
Library of Congess/public domain and under license
from © Shutterstock.com other than the following:
Regency House Publishing Limited: 7, 72-73, 74-75.

The content of this book was first published as
CIVIL WAR.

ABOUT THE AUTHOR
Johnathan Sutherland & Diane Canwell
Together, Diane Canwell and Jonathan Sutherland are
the authors of 150 books, and have written
extensively about the American Civil War. Both
have a particular interest in American history, and its
military aspects in particular. Several of their books
have attracted prizes and awards, including New York
Library's Best of Reference and Book List's
Editor's Choice.